WINNER'S PLAYBOOK

(A COLLECTION OF ESSAYS ON VICTORY)

ESSAY ONE

BY

MICHAEL NORDMAN

ESSAY ONE

ISBN: 979-8-9959169-0-1

UNITED STATES

For the love of Christ

If someone thinks their perspective of what the Bible says is unimpeachable and that there is no way that they are perhaps missing something, you would have to ask, “Do they know what the Mystery is?”. The Mystery of Christ in you! This is the cornerstone of Christianity and always has been.

A cornerstone is foundational.

The weird thing is that this biblical concept of truth, about the MYSTERY – CHRIST IN YOU, has been lost to the general population of the Church. When was the last time you heard someone talk about “the” Mystery? Why is that?

Let’s explore the riches of the glory of the mystery, which is the foundation of the Church and the fulfillment of the Word of God which the Apostle writes about in the Letter to the saints and faithful brethren in Colosse, sometime[①]. Maybe other things are BUILT upon it.

IF you can't honestly challenge a doctrine which is held by your group and/or the perspective which they have about it (which is mandatory for your participation in that group), with Scripture and an illumination by the Holy Spirit, without getting kicked out... Even if billions of people are in that group and they are thoroughly convinced that their take on everything is correct, maybe it is time.

① To whom God would make known what is the riches of the glory of this mystery among the Gentiles; which is Christ in you, the hope of glory. Colossians 1:27 KJV

Unity is based on truth.

As we discuss in other essays, the only way you will know **"THE TRUTH"** which sets you free is by being **A DISCIPLE OF JESUS CHRIST.**

Often times a whole system of error will hinge on just one little perspective*, which is contrary to the intent of Scripture,* in its foundation. Then other things will get twisted up to fit with that narrative. This is how cults, divisions, and false religions are spawned, grow, and established.

Obviously today there is a wide array of perspectives to choose from. Why is that?

The unique thing about being deceived is that you don't even know it.

HOW CAN YOU KNOW IT?

You will never know it unless you objectively (or honestly, independent of your affiliation) challenge the core premise of whatever perspective has been presented to you with God's perspective. Then, if that perspective is right, you will know it. If that perspective is off, you will have the opportunity to discover the right one.

For our exhortation was not of deceit,
nor of uncleanness, nor in guile:
4 But as we were allowed of God
to be put in trust with the gospel,
even so we speak; not as pleasing men,

but God, which trieth our hearts.
5 For neither at any time used we
flattering words, as ye know,
nor a cloke of covetousness;
God is witness:
6 Nor of men sought we glory,
neither of you, nor yet of others,
when we might have been burdensome,
as the apostles of Christ.

1 Thessalonians 2:3-6 KJV

This is what real apostles, prophets, evangelists, pastors, and teachers do.

Let's see what the Bible says about the purpose of apostles, prophets, evangelists, pastors, and teachers. **REAL TALK!**

For the perfecting of the saints,
for the work of the ministry,
for the edifying of the body of Christ:
Till we all come in the unity of the faith,
and of the knowledge of the Son of God,
unto a perfect man,
unto the measure of the stature
of the fulness of Christ:
That we henceforth be no more children,
tossed to and fro,
and carried about with every wind of doctrine,
by the sleight of men,
and cunning craftiness,
whereby they lie in wait to deceive;
But speaking the truth in love,
may grow up into him in all things,
which is the head, even Christ:

Ephesians 4:12-15 (KJV)

In order that we may be no longer babes,
tossed and carried about
by every wind of *that* teaching
[which is] in the sleight of men,
in unprincipled cunning
with a view to systematized error;
Ephesians 4:14-15 (DARBY)

Someone does not have to be intentionally misleading you. Most likely, they think they are doing the right thing for God. They just don't understand what they are doing②. Yet, they continue to do it.

Next, we can obviously see what Jesus is doing in his church, today, as always. Just look and see.

And he (Jesus) gave the apostles, the prophets, the
evangelists, the shepherds and teachers, [12] to equip③
the saints for the work of ministry, for building up the
body of Christ, [13] until we all attain to the unity of the
faith and of the knowledge of the Son of God, to
mature manhood, to the measure of the stature of
the fullness of Christ, [14] so that we may no longer be
children, tossed to and fro by the waves and carried
about by every wind of doctrine, by human cunning,

② For I bear them record that they have a zeal of God, but not according to knowledge. [3] For they being ignorant of God's righteousness, and going about to establish their own righteousness, have not submitted themselves unto the righteousness of God. Romans 10:3 KJV

③ The Greek word for "equip" is the same word used for fishermen mending their nets. The job of the ministries is to repair the saints from the damage caused by the systematizing of error or deceitful schemes and help them grow up.

by craftiness in deceitful schemes. [15] Rather, speaking the truth in love, we are to grow up in every way into him who is the head, into Christ, [16] from whom the whole body, joined and held together by every joint with which it is equipped, when each part is working properly, makes the body grow so that it builds itself up in love.

Ephesians 4:11-16 ESV

It would just make sense to be in sync with Jesus and what he is doing. That's the road to **VICTORY!**

I love you.

HOW DO WE DO THIS?

THE SAME WAY THEY DID IT IN THE FIRST CENTURY!

LIKE IT SAYS IN THE BOOK OF ACTS.

These were more noble than those in Thessalonica,
in that they received the word
with all readiness of mind,
and searched the scriptures daily,
whether those things were so.

Acts 17:11 (KJV)

If the saints were supposed to check, even what an apostle was saying or teaching with Scripture, how much more is it a good thing for us to do today?

If you are a baptized member of the Body of Christ, the reason you were baptized is to be a disciple of Jesus Christ and to learn and obey all that he taught.

And Jesus came and said to them, "All authority in heaven and on earth has been given to me. [19] Go therefore and make disciples of all nations, baptizing them in the name of the Father and of the Son and of the Holy Spirit, [20] teaching them to observe all that I have commanded you. And behold, I am with you always, to the end of the age."

Matthew 28:18-20 (ESV)

To be Jesus's disciple It begins with love. You love, you keep his word, and you bear much fruit. It begins with the basics and then continues with the basics. You just get better at the basics. They are all a priority. Keeping his word is a priority. What does it mean to keep his word? It means you keep it from corruption. You keep it in the same condition as it was originally spoken by Jesus himself. **You respect it**. This is what the apostles and prophets did. They had the help of the Holy Spirit. They had the inspiration and revelation from the Holy Spirit to reveal the MYSTERY and write the New Testament.

We also have the Holy Spirit to guide us through and teach us what these words mean… to open the eyes of our hearts to discover, realize, and understand the spiritual realities and the things Jesus was talking about, as they are unfolded for us in Holy Scripture. This is **HOW** we do it.

Pray and read the Bible. Ask God to teach you and He will. You will know it is God when you see it clearly in Scripture, rightly divided, not with man's philosophy and empty deceit but with the anointing of God teaching you.

ILLUMINATION OF SCRIPTURE

As we can see, the Apostle John understood this lost art of receiving and understanding by the Spirit and declares that it is for you.

But the anointing that you received from him abides in you, and you have no need that anyone should teach you. But as his anointing teaches you about everything, and is true, and is no lie—just as it has taught you, abide in him.

1 John 2:27

The Apostle Paul and the saints experienced it.

Which things also we speak,
not in the words
which man's wisdom teacheth,
but which the Holy Ghost teacheth;
comparing spiritual things with
spiritual.

1 Corinthians 2:13

There are many other ***Bible verses*** which say the same thing or indirectly imply this same truth about the Holy Spirit being our Teacher, now-a-days. There is no doubt about it.

WHAT ABOUT YOU?

It is quite available to you too. You can do it!

Jesus quoted the Old Testament about it.

It is written in the Prophets,
'And they will all be taught by God.' Everyone who has heard and learned from the Father comes to me.
John 6:45

You can get started any time you want.

Here is a prayer you can say.

Abba Father,

I pray that I get it.
I ask that You
open the eyes of my heart
so, I can see…
that the revelation of the Mystery
of Christ in Me,
and the Gospel of Grace,
be illuminated in me,
that You give me understanding
of Your will
and engage with me as I read
and meditate on Your Holy Scripture,
written to me.

In the Name of Jesus, Amen.

The Holy Spirit unlocks the Faith of Christ in Holy Scriptures into your heart, and the Life of Christ is manifested in your soul. This is how we are transformed. This is how we engage our spirit through prayer while reading Scripture. All the benefits, blessings, favor, power, prayers, and standards written in the books of the Bible written to you are yours.

Jesus foretold that it would be for you.

But the Helper, the Holy Spirit,
whom the Father will send in my name,
he will teach you all things
and bring to your remembrance
all that I have said to you.
John 14:26

Read what Jesus said about the Holy Spirit.

And I say unto you, Ask, and it shall be given
you; seek, and ye shall find; knock,
and it shall be opened unto you.
10 For every one that asks receives; and he that
seeks finds; and to him that knocks
it shall be opened.
11 If a son shall ask bread of any of you that is a
father, will he give him a stone? or if *he ask* a
fish, will he for a fish give him a serpent?
12 Or if he shall ask an egg,
will he offer him a scorpion?

[13] If ye then, being evil, know how to give good gifts unto your children, how much more shall *your* heavenly Father
give the Holy Spirit to those that ask him?

Luke 11:9-13 KJV

LOOK FOR FUTURE ESSAYS

ON

VICTORY

WEAREUNDERGRACE.COM

OR

AMAZON

AND please(!)

TELL YOUR FRIENDS

BIBLIOGRAPHY

Special thanks to the Holy Spirit of the Living God who inspired this essay and opens the eyes of our heart.

The ESV Bible (The Holy Bible, English Standard Version®), © 2001

Interlinear Bible from Bible Hub @ biblehub.com.

Public Domain: King James Version **(KJV),** Darby Translation **(DARBY).**

ART CREDITS

DREAMSTIME.COM

108985629 © Sergeypykhonin
Surfer-riding-blue-wave-mentawai-indonesia-image ID 10434862 © Photogerson
Woman-looking-large-book-image ID 28421011 © Kevin Carden
Warm-atmosphere-cute-woman-expressing-positivity-spending-her-break-pleasure-cheerful-brunette-girl-reading-favorite-image ID 167193646 © Viacheslav Iacobchuk
Attractive-european-womam-thought-cloud-portrait-thoughtful-young-european-woman-thought-cloud-standing-concrete-image ID 122494779 © Peshkova (Modified for cloud use)
Greeting-card-flower-lace-white-pink-background-place-your-text-vector-illustration-beautiful-flowers-image ID 73042336 © Svagaa

CRAIYON

Babies in the Ocean_140054_

SHUTTERSTOCK

1763027240 GLOWING BIBLE SHUTTERSTOCK Romolo Tavani
1862538154 WOMAN WITH QUESTION MARKS Tanya
2138118693 FIGURES ZayacSK

MICHAEL NORDMAN

COVER ART

www.ingramcontent.com/pod-product-compliance
Lightning Source LLC
LaVergne TN
LVHW052311100826
845147LV00006B/730

9798995916901